Fun Stuff

Silly Snacks

Publications International, Ltd.

Some of the products listed in this publication may be in limited distribution.

Front cover photography and photography on pages 5, 7, 9, 11, 21, 25, 27, 31, 41, 47, 53, 65, 69, 71, 79, 83, 89, 95, 103 and 115 by Laurie Proffitt Photography, Chicago.
Photographer: Laurie Proffitt
Photographer's Assistant: Chad Evans
Food Stylist: Carol Smoler
Assistant Food Stylist: Elaine Funk

Pictured on the front cover *(clockwise from top left):* Mini Dizzy Dogs *(page 8)*, Pig-wich *(page 94)*, Tiny Shrimp Tacos with Peach Salsa *(page 26)* and Friendly Face Pizzas *(page 82)*.
Pictured on the jacket flaps: Snake Snacks *(page 78)* and Bavarian Pretzel Sandwich *(page 70)*.
Pictured on the back cover *(left to right):* Porky Pinwheels *(page 52)*, Guacamole Cones *(page 68)* and Meat Loaf Cupcakes *(page 6)*.

ISBN-13: 978-1-60553-317-9
ISBN-10: 1-60553-317-3

Library of Congress Control Number: 2009935781

Manufactured in China.

8 7 6 5 4 3 2 1

Microwave Cooking: Microwave ovens vary in wattage. Use the cooking times as guidelines and check for doneness before adding more time.

Preparation/Cooking Times: Preparation times are based on the approximate amount of time required to assemble the recipe before cooking, baking, chilling or serving. These times include preparation steps such as measuring, chopping and mixing. The fact that some preparations and cooking can be done simultaneously is taken into account. Preparation of optional ingredients and serving suggestions is not included.

 Publications International, Ltd.

Contents

Reinvented Classics

Mac and Cheese Mini Cups

3 tablespoons butter, divided
2 tablespoons all-purpose flour
1 cup milk
1 teaspoon salt
½ teaspoon black pepper
1 cup (4 ounces) shredded sharp Cheddar cheese
1 cup (4 ounces) shredded Muenster cheese
½ pound uncooked elbow macaroni, cooked and drained
⅓ cup toasted bread crumbs

1. Preheat oven to 400°F. Melt 1 tablespoon butter in small saucepan over low heat. Grease 36 mini (1¾-inch) muffin cups with melted butter.

2. Melt remaining 2 tablespoons butter in large saucepan over medium heat. Whisk in flour; cook 2 minutes. Add milk, salt and pepper; cook and stir 3 minutes or until mixture is thickened. Remove from heat; stir in cheeses. Fold in macaroni.

3. Divide macaroni and cheese among prepared muffin cups. Top with toasted bread crumbs.

4. Bake 20 to 25 minutes or until golden brown. Cool 10 minutes in pans; remove carefully using sharp knife.

Makes 36 appetizers

Meat Loaf Cupcakes

   3 medium potatoes, peeled and chopped
1½ pounds 90% lean ground beef
  ½ cup finely chopped onion
  ⅓ cup old-fashioned oats
   1 egg
   2 tablespoons chopped fresh rosemary
  ½ cup milk
   2 tablespoons butter
   1 teaspoon salt
     Black pepper
  ¼ cup snipped chives

1. Preheat oven to 350°F. Place potatoes in medium saucepan; cover with water. Bring to a boil; cook 25 to 30 minutes or until potatoes are fork-tender.

2. Meanwhile, combine beef, onion, oats, egg and rosemary in large bowl; mix well. Divide mixture among 10 standard (2½-inch) muffin cups. Bake 25 minutes or until cooked through (145°F).

3. Beat potatoes, milk, butter, salt and pepper in large bowl with electric mixer at medium speed 3 minutes or until smooth. Place potato mixture in large piping bag fitted with large star tip.

4. Remove meat loaf cupcakes to serving platter. Pipe mashed potatoes on top for frosting. Sprinkle with chives.   *Makes 10 servings*

Meat Loaf Cupcakes

Mini Dizzy Dogs

½ sheet (8-ounce can) refrigerated crescent roll dough
20 mini hot dogs or smoked sausages
Ketchup and mustard

1. Preheat oven to 375°F. Line baking sheet with parchment paper.

2. Slice dough rectangle lengthwise into 20 (¼-inch) strips. Coil 1 dough strip around 1 hot dog. Place onto prepared baking sheet. Repeat with remaining dough strips and hot dogs.

3. Bake 10 to 12 minutes or until light golden brown. Serve with ketchup and mustard for dipping.
Makes 20 appetizers

Sloppy Joe Sliders

12 ounces 90% lean ground beef
1 can (about 14 ounces) stewed tomatoes with Mexican seasonings
½ cup frozen mixed vegetables, thawed
½ cup chopped green bell pepper
3 tablespoons ketchup
2 teaspoons Worcestershire sauce
1 teaspoon ground cumin
1 teaspoon cider vinegar
24 mini whole wheat rolls, split and warmed

1. Brown ground beef in large nonstick skillet over medium-high heat, stirring to break up meat; drain fat.

2. Add tomatoes, mixed vegetables, bell pepper, ketchup, Worcestershire, cumin and vinegar; bring to a boil. Reduce heat; cover and simmer 15 minutes or until peppers are tender and mixture has thickened. Break up large pieces of tomato.

3. To serve, spoon 2 tablespoons meat mixture onto each bun.
Makes 24 mini sandwiches

Mini Dizzy Dogs

BLT Biscuits

2 cups all-purpose flour
2 teaspoons sugar
2 teaspoons baking powder
1 teaspoon black pepper
½ teaspoon baking soda
½ teaspoon salt
⅓ cup cold butter, cut into small pieces
1 cup (4 ounces) shredded Cheddar cheese
¾ cup buttermilk
1 package (16 ounces) bacon slices, cooked
1 small head romaine lettuce
4 plum tomatoes
½ cup mayonnaise

1. Preheat oven to 425°F. Line baking sheets with parchment paper.

2. Combine flour, sugar, baking powder, pepper, baking soda and salt in large bowl. Cut in butter with pastry blender or two knives until mixture resembles coarse crumbs. Stir in cheese and buttermilk just until mixture forms dough.

3. Turn dough out onto lightly floured surface; knead gently several times. Pat into 8×6-inch rectangle (about ¾ inch thick). Cut dough into 24 squares with sharp knife; place on prepared baking sheets. Bake 10 to 12 minutes or until golden brown. Cool slightly on wire rack.

4. Cut each bacon slice into 3 pieces. Tear lettuce into small pieces to fit on biscuits. Cut tomatoes into ¼-inch slices.

5. Split biscuits; spread each half lightly with mayonnaise. Layer each biscuit with 2 slices bacon, lettuce and 1 slice tomato.

Makes 24 mini sandwiches

Turkey Club Biscuits: Prepare BLT Biscuits as directed above, adding deli sliced turkey and avocado slices.

BLT Biscuits

Hawaiian Pizza Bites

    1 canister (13.9 ounce) refrigerated pizza crust dough
    ¾ cup pizza sauce
    1½ cups (6 ounce) shredded mozzarella cheese
    3 ounce sliced Canadian bacon, cut into small pieces
    1 can (8 ounces) DOLE® Pineapple Tidbits *or* 1 can (20 ounce) DOLE® Pineapple
        Chunks, drained

• Unroll dough onto lightly floured surface. Cut 15 to 16 circles with 3-inch cookie or biscuit cutter and place them on cookie sheet sprayed with nonstick vegetable cooking spray.

• Bake at 400°F., 8 minutes. Remove from oven. Top crusts with pizza sauce, one-half cheese, Canadian bacon and pineapple tidbits. Top with remaining cheese.

• Bake an additional 6 to 10 minutes or until crusts are golden brown.

Makes 15 to 16 pizza bites

Prep Time: 10 minutes
Bake Time: 18 minutes

Tip A couple of these tasty pizzas would be a welcome addition to any lunchbox!

Hawaiian Pizza Bites

Micro Mini Stuffed Potatoes

 1 pound small new red potatoes
¼ cup sour cream
 2 tablespoons butter, softened
½ teaspoon minced garlic
¼ cup milk
½ cup (2 ounces) shredded sharp Cheddar cheese
½ teaspoon salt
¼ teaspoon black pepper
¼ cup finely chopped green onions (optional)

Microwave Directions

1. Pierce potatoes with fork in several places. Microwave potatoes on HIGH 5 to 6 minutes or until tender. Let stand 5 minutes; cut in half lengthwise. Scoop out pulp from potatoes and place in medium bowl. Set potato shells aside.

2. Beat potato pulp with electric mixer at low speed 30 seconds. Add sour cream, butter and garlic; beat until well blended. Gradually add milk, beating until smooth. Add cheese, salt and pepper; beat until blended.

3. Fill each potato shell with equal amounts of potato mixture. Microwave on HIGH 1 to 2 minutes or until cheese melts. Garnish with green onions. *Makes 4 servings*

Micro Mini Stuffed Potatoes

Croque Monsieur Bites

8 thin slices firm sandwich bread
4 slices Swiss cheese, halved (about 4 ounces)
4 slices smoked ham (about 4 ounces)
   Dash grated nutmeg
2 tablespoons butter, melted

1. Cut crusts from bread. Place 4 slices bread on work surface. Layer each with half slice cheese, 1 slice ham and remaining half slice cheese; sprinkle with nutmeg. Top with remaining 4 slices bread. Brush outside of sandwiches with melted butter.

2. Cook sandwiches in large skillet over medium heat 2 to 3 minutes per side or until golden brown and cheese is melted. Cut into quarters.

Makes 16 pieces

 Tip These sandwiches can be prepared ahead of time and reheated for an easy party appetizer. Leave sandwiches whole after cooking and refrigerate until ready to serve. Cut into quarters and place on foil-lined baking sheet; bake in preheated 350°F oven about 8 minutes or until sandwiches are heated through and cheese is melted.

Croque Monsieur Bites

Soft Pretzels

1¼ cups milk
4 to 4½ cups all-purpose flour, divided
¼ cup sugar
1 package active dry yeast
1 teaspoon baking powder
1 teaspoon garlic salt
½ cup (1 stick) unsalted butter, melted
2 tablespoons baking soda
Coarse salt, sesame seeds or poppy seeds

1. Heat milk in small saucepan over low heat to 105° to 115°F.

2. Beat 3 cups flour, sugar, yeast, baking powder and garlic salt in large bowl with dough hook of electric mixer at low speed. Add milk and butter; beat vigorously 2 minutes. Add remaining flour, ¼ cup at a time, until dough begins to pull away from side of bowl.

3. Turn dough out onto lightly floured surface; flatten slightly. Knead 10 minutes or until smooth and elastic, adding flour if necessary to prevent sticking.

4. Shape dough into ball. Place in large, lightly oiled bowl; turn dough to grease top. Cover with towel; let rise in warm place about 30 minutes.

5. Divide dough into 18 equal pieces. Roll each piece into 22-inch-long rope on lightly oiled surface. Form each rope into U shape. About 2 inches from each end, cross dough. Fold loose ends down to rounded part of U; press ends to seal. Turn pretzels over so that ends are on bottom and reshape if necessary. Cover with towel; let rest 20 minutes.

6. Preheat oven to 400°F. Grease baking sheets or line with parchment paper. Fill large Dutch oven three-fourths full with water. Bring to a boil over high heat. Add baking soda. Carefully drop pretzels, 3 at a time, into boiling water for 10 seconds. Remove with slotted spoon. Place on prepared baking sheets. Sprinkle with coarse salt, sesame seeds or poppy seeds.

7. Bake 15 minutes or until golden brown. Place on wire racks; cool completely.

Makes 18 large pretzels

Soft Pretzels

Grilled Cheese Kabobs

8 thick slices whole wheat bread
3 thick slices sharp Cheddar cheese
3 thick slices Monterey Jack or Colby Jack cheese
2 tablespoons butter, melted

1. Cut each slice of bread into 1-inch squares. Cut each slice of cheese into 1-inch squares. Make small sandwiches with 1 square of bread and 1 square of each type of cheese. Top with second square of bread.

2. Place sandwiches on the end of short wooden skewers. Brush 4 sides of sandwiches with melted butter.

3. Heat nonstick grill pan over medium-high heat. Grill sandwich kabobs 30 seconds on each of 4 sides or until golden and cheese is slightly melted. *Makes 12 servings*

Tuna Schooners

1 can (6 ounces) tuna packed in water, drained and flaked
½ cup finely chopped apple
¼ cup shredded carrot
⅓ cup ranch salad dressing
2 English muffins, split and lightly toasted
8 triangular-shaped tortilla chips

1. Combine tuna, apple and carrot in medium bowl. Add salad dressing; mix well.

2. Spread one fourth of tuna mixture on top of each muffin half.

3. Stand 2 crackers and press firmly into tuna mixture to form sails. *Makes 4 servings*

Grilled Cheese Kabobs

Popcorn & Pretzel Sweet Snack Mix

REYNOLDS® Parchment Paper
1 bag (2.9 ounces) microwave low-fat popcorn
2 cups mini pretzels
1 cup coarsely chopped roasted almonds
1 cup coarsely chopped sweetened dried cranberries
1 bag (12 ounces) white chocolate chips
1½ teaspoons ground cinnamon

LINE a 15½×10×1-inch baking pan or large tray with Reynolds Parchment Paper; set aside.

POP popcorn according to package directions; shake bag so that un-popped kernels fall to the bottom.

POUR popcorn, pretzels, almonds and dried cranberries into a large bowl. Discard un-popped popcorn kernels.

MELT white chocolate chips following package directions. Stir in cinnamon until well blended; pour over popcorn mixture. Toss to evenly coat.

SPREAD mixture evenly in parchment-lined pan. Let stand at room temperature to harden, about 1 hour. Break apart large pieces. Store in airtight container.   *Makes 11 cups*

Prep Time: 10 minutes
Cook Time: 3 minutes

Popcorn & Pretzel Sweet Snack Mix

Italian Chicken Nuggets

¼ cup all-purpose flour
1 egg, lightly beaten
1 cup toasted bread crumbs
½ cup grated Parmesan cheese
2 teaspoons dried Italian seasoning
  Salt and black pepper
3 boneless skinless chicken breasts, cut into 1-inch pieces
  Olive oil cooking spray
  Warm pasta sauce

1. Preheat oven to 400°F. Line baking sheet with parchment paper.

2. Place flour in shallow bowl. Place egg in second shallow bowl. Combine bread crumbs, cheese, Italian seasoning, salt and pepper in third shallow bowl.

3. Dip each piece of chicken into flour, then in egg, then roll in bread crumb mixture. Place on prepared baking sheet. Spray chicken with cooking spray.

4. Bake for 25 minutes or until nuggets are browned and cooked through. Serve with warm pasta sauce for dipping.

Makes 4 servings

Tip Need a break from chicken? Cubed pork tenderloin would be an outstanding substitute!

Italian Chicken Nuggets

Game's On!

Tiny Shrimp Tacos with Peach Salsa

1 peach, peeled and finely diced
2 tablespoons finely chopped red onion
1 small jalapeño pepper,* finely chopped
  Juice of 1 lime
1 tablespoon chopped fresh parsley or cilantro
1 clove garlic, minced
½ teaspoon salt
8 (6-inch) flour tortillas
1 tablespoon vegetable oil
1 pound medium raw shrimp, peeled, deveined and cut into small pieces
2 teaspoons chili powder

Jalapeño peppers can sting and irritate the skin, so wear rubber gloves when handling peppers and do not touch your eyes.

1. Combine peach, onion, jalapeño, lime juice, parsley, garlic and salt in medium nonreactive bowl. Set aside.

2. Preheat oven to 400°F. Cut out 24 (2½-inch) tortilla rounds using cookie cutter or sharp knife. Discard scraps. Place tortilla rounds over handle of wooden spoon; secure with toothpicks. Bake 5 minutes; repeat with remaining tortilla rounds.

3. Heat oil in large nonstick skillet over medium-high heat. Add shrimp and chili powder; cook and stir 3 minutes or until shrimp are pink and opaque.

4. Place a few shrimp pieces in each taco shell; top each taco with peach salsa.

Makes 24 tacos

Guacamole Sliders

1 ripe avocado
1 tablespoon ORTEGA® Fire-Roasted Diced Green Chiles
1 tablespoon chopped cilantro
1 tablespoon lime juice
⅛ teaspoon salt
1 pound lean ground beef
1 tablespoon water
1 cup ORTEGA® Garden Vegetable Salsa, Medium, divided
12 dinner rolls

Cut avocado in half and remove pit. Scoop out avocado with spoon and place in small bowl. Add chiles, cilantro, lime juice and salt. Gently mash with fork until blended; set aside.

Combine beef, water and ½ cup salsa in medium bowl. Form mixture into 12 small round balls. Flatten slightly.

Grill or pan-fry burgers about 3 minutes. Turn over and flatten with spatula. Cook 4 minutes longer or until desired doneness.

Cut each roll in half. Fill with 1 tablespoon remaining salsa, 1 burger and 1 heaping tablespoon guacamole. Serve immediately. *Makes 12 small burgers*

Tip: Try using a panini press or similar double-sided grill to cook the sliders even faster.

Prep Time: 10 minutes
Start to Finish: 20 minutes

Guacamole Sliders

Buffalo Wedges

3 pounds Yukon Gold potatoes
3 tablespoons hot pepper sauce
2 tablespoons butter, melted
2 teaspoons smoked or sweet paprika
Blue cheese dressing

1. Preheat oven to 400°F. Spray baking sheet with nonstick cooking spray. Slice potatoes into 4 or 6 wedges, depending on size of potato.

2. Combine hot pepper sauce, butter and paprika in large bowl. Add potato wedges; toss to coat well. Place wedges in single layer on prepared baking sheet.

3. Bake 20 minutes. Flip potatoes; bake 20 minutes or until light golden brown and crisp. Serve with blue cheese dressing.

Makes 4 servings

Poblano Pepper Kabobs

1 large poblano pepper*
4 ounces smoked turkey breast, cut into 8 cubes
4 ounces pepper jack cheese, cut into 8 cubes
¼ cup salsa (optional)

*Poblano peppers can sting and irritate the skin, so wear rubber gloves when handling peppers and do not touch your eyes.

1. Preheat oven to 400°F. Soak 4 wooden skewers in warm water 20 minutes to prevent burning.

2. Meanwhile, fill medium saucepan half full with water; bring to a boil over medium-high heat. Add pepper; cook for 1 minute. Drain. Core, seed and cut pepper into 12 bite-size pieces. Thread 1 piece pepper, 1 piece turkey and 1 piece cheese onto each skewer. Repeat, ending with pepper.

3. Place kabobs on baking sheet. Bake 3 minutes or until cheese starts to melt. Remove immediately. Serve with salsa, if desired.

Makes 4 servings

Buffalo Wedges

Velveeta® Double-Decker Nachos

    6 ounces tortilla chips (about 7 cups)
    1 can (15 ounces) chili with beans
    ½ pound (8 ounces) VELVEETA® Pasteurized Prepared Cheese Product,
        cut into ½-inch cubes
    1 medium tomato, finely chopped
    ¼ cup sliced green onions
    ⅓ cup BREAKSTONE'S® or KNUDSEN® Sour Cream

Arrange half of the chips on large microwaveable platter; top with layers of half each of the chili and VELVEETA®. Repeat layers.

Microwave on High 3 to 5 minutes or until VELVEETA® is melted.

Top with remaining ingredients.   *Makes 6 servings*

Size-Wise: Enjoy your favorite foods while keeping portion size in mind.

Substitute: Prepare as directed, using VELVEETA® Mild Mexican Pasteurized Prepared Cheese Product with Jalapeño Peppers.

Prep Time: 15 minutes
Total Time: 15 minutes

Velveeta® Double-Decker Nachos

Super Bowl Snack Mix

½ cup packed brown sugar
1 teaspoon chili powder
½ teaspoon salt
½ teaspoon curry powder
½ teaspoon five-spice powder
1½ cups raw almonds
1 cup dried cherries
1 cup shelled raw pistachio nuts
1 egg white

1. Preheat oven to 250°F.

2. Combine brown sugar, chili powder, salt, curry powder and five-spice powder in medium bowl; stir well. Add almonds, cherries and pistachios; mix well.

3. Whisk egg white in large bowl until frothy. Add almond mixture; toss to combine.

4. Spread mixture evenly onto nonstick baking sheet. Bake 35 to 40 minutes, stirring occasionally. Let mixture cool 30 minutes or until coating is firm. Break into small chunks. Store mix in airtight container.

Makes 14 servings

Super Bowl Snack Mix

Pizza Fries

1 bag (2 pounds) frozen French fries
1 cup PREGO® Traditional Italian Sauce, any variety
1½ cups shredded mozzarella cheese (about 6 ounces)
Diced pepperoni (optional)

1. Prepare the fries according to the package directions. Remove from the oven. Pour the sauce over the fries.

2. Top with the cheese and pepperoni, if desired.

3. Bake for 5 minutes or until the cheese is melted.

Makes 8 servings

Prep Time: 20 minutes
Bake Time: 5 minutes

Tip Check out the tasty variety of French fries in the freezer case. Waffle cut, seasoned or even tots would be perfect for this silly snack.

Pizza Fries

Baked Pork Buns

　　1 tablespoon vegetable oil
　　2 cups coarsely chopped bok choy
　　1 small onion or large shallot, thinly sliced
　　1 container (18 ounces) refrigerated shredded barbecue pork
　　2 containers (10 ounces each) refrigerated buttermilk biscuit dough

1. Preheat oven to 350°F. Grease baking sheets.

2. Heat oil in large skillet over medium-high heat. Add bok choy and onion; cook and stir 8 to 10 minutes or until vegetables are tender. Remove from heat; stir in barbecue pork.

3. Lightly dust work surface with flour. Remove biscuits from containers and separate into individual biscuits. Split 1 biscuit in half crosswise to create two thin biscuits. Roll each biscuit half into 5-inch circle.

4. Spoon heaping tablespoon pork mixture onto one side of circle. Fold dough over filling to form half circle; press edges to seal. Arrange buns on prepared baking sheet. Repeat with remaining biscuits and filling. Bake 12 to 15 minutes or until golden brown.　　*Makes 20 buns*

Baked Pork Buns

Chili Cheese Mini Dogs

  2 teaspoons chili powder
  ½ sheet (8 ounce can) refrigerated crescent roll dough
  5 slices sharp Cheddar cheese
20 mini hot dogs

1. Preheat oven to 375°F. Line baking sheet with parchment paper.

2. Sprinkle 1 teaspoon chili powder evenly over each side of dough. Cut dough into 20 squares.

3. Cut each cheese slice into 4 squares. Press 1 cheese square onto 1 dough square. Place 1 hot dog in center; bring up sides of dough to secure hot dog. Place onto prepared baking sheet. Repeat with remaining cheese, dough and hot dogs.

4. Bake 12 minutes or until dough is golden brown. *Makes 20 servings*

Hot Cheesy Chili Dip

  1 pound lean ground beef
  ½ cup chopped onion
  1 package (1 pound) pasteurized process cheese spread with jalapeño pepper,
     cut into cubes
  1 can (15 ounces) kidney beans, drained
  1 bottle (12 ounces) HEINZ® Chili Sauce
  ¼ cup chopped fresh parsley
    Tortilla chips or crackers

In large saucepan, cook beef and onion until onion is tender; drain. Stir in cheese, beans and chili sauce; heat, stirring until cheese is melted. Stir in parsley. Serve warm with tortilla chips or crackers. Makes about 5 cups

Chili Cheese Mini Dogs

Beer-Braised Meatballs

  1 pound ground beef
  ½ cup Italian bread crumbs
  ½ cup grated Parmesan cheese
  2 eggs, lightly beaten
  ⅓ cup finely chopped onion
  2 cloves garlic, minced
  ½ teaspoon black pepper
  ¼ teaspoon salt
  1 bottle (12 ounces) light-colored beer, such as lager
1½ cups tomato sauce
  1 cup ketchup
  ½ cup packed brown sugar
  2 tablespoons tomato paste

1. Preheat oven to 400°F. Line broiler pan with foil; spray rack with nonstick cooking spray. Combine beef, bread crumbs, cheese, eggs, onion, garlic, pepper and salt in large bowl; shape mixture into 1-inch balls.

2. Place meatballs on broiler rack. Bake 10 minutes or until browned.

3. Bring beer, tomato sauce, ketchup, sugar and tomato paste to a boil in Dutch oven. Add meatballs and reduce heat. Cover; cook and stir 20 to 30 minutes or until meatballs are cooked through.

Makes 20 meatballs

Beer-Braised Meatballs

Cream Cheese Nibbles

  1 package (8 ounces) PHILADELPHIA® Cream Cheese
½ cup KRAFT® Sun-Dried Tomato Dressing
  2 cloves garlic, sliced
  3 small sprigs fresh rosemary, stems removed
  6 sprigs fresh thyme, cut into pieces
  1 teaspoon black peppercorns
    Peel of 1 lemon, cut into thin strips

CUT cream cheese into 36 pieces. Place in 9-inch pie plate.

ADD remaining ingredients; toss lightly. Cover.

REFRIGERATE at least 1 hour or up to 24 hours. Serve with crusty bread, NABISCO® Crackers or pita chips.
Makes 18 servings, 2 pieces each

Prep Time: 10 minutes plus refrigerating

Zesty Buffalo Style Popcorn

  3 tablespoons hot pepper jelly
  1 teaspoon Cajun seasoning
  1 tablespoon zero-calorie margarine cooking spray
  1 bag (3 ounces) JOLLY TIME® Healthy Pop 94% Fat Free Microwave Popcorn, popped
20 baked ranch-flavored crackers
16 reduced-fat cheese snack crackers

1. In a small bowl, combine jelly, Cajun seasoning and margarine spray; mix well.

2. Place popped popcorn in a large bowl, removing any unpopped kernels. Add ranch and cheese crackers, toss to combine. Drizzle with jelly mixture. Transfer to two 9-inch microwave-safe pie pans. Microwave each on high for 1½ minutes, stirring halfway through cooking time.

3. Transfer to waxed paper to cool.
Makes 9 servings

Prep Time: 10 minutes

·Game's On!·

Cream Cheese Nibbles

Zucchinidillas

Nonstick cooking spray
1 tablespoon vegetable oil
1 zucchini, thinly sliced
½ cup thinly sliced red onion
⅔ cup green salsa, divided
½ cup (2 ounces) shredded Cheddar cheese
½ cup (2 ounces) shredded Monterey jack cheese
6 (6-inch) flour tortillas, divided
½ cup sour cream

1. Preheat oven to 400°F. Line baking sheet with foil. Spray with cooking spray.

2. Heat oil in medium skillet over medium-high heat. Add zucchini and onion; cook and stir 5 minutes or until vegetables are softened. Stir in ⅓ cup salsa; remove from heat. Stir in cheeses.

3. Place 3 tortillas on baking sheet. Divide zucchini mixture among tortillas. Top with remaining 3 tortillas. Spray top tortillas with cooking spray. Bake 8 minutes or until cheese is melted and tortillas are crisp.

4. Combine sour cream and remaining ⅓ cup salsa in small bowl. Cut quesadillas into wedges; serve with sour cream mixture.

Makes 4 to 6 servings

Zucchinidillas

Mini Reuben Skewers with Dipping Sauce

⅓ cup HELLMANN'S® or BEST FOODS® Real Mayonnaise
⅓ cup WISH-BONE® Thousand Island Dressing
 1 can (8 ounces) sauerkraut, drained and coarsely chopped
 4 thin slices rye bread, crust removed
 8 ounces sliced Swiss cheese
 8 ounces sliced cooked corned beef or pastrami

1. Combine HELLMANN'S® or BEST FOODS® Real Mayonnaise, WISH-BONE® Thousand Island Dressing and sauerkraut in medium bowl; set aside.

2. Top 2 bread slices evenly with cheese, corned beef, then remaining bread. Cut each sandwich into 20 cubes and secure with wooden toothpicks. Serve with dipping sauce.

Makes 40 servings

Prep Time: 10 minutes

 *Tip* Stock up on fun toothpicks from party stores and catalogs. They can liven up any party treat!

Mini Reuben Skewers with Dipping Sauce

Roasted Red Potato Bites

1½ pounds red potatoes (about 15 small)
  1 cup shredded Cheddar cheese (about 4 ounces)
 ½ cup HELLMANN'S® or BEST FOODS® Real Mayonnaise
 ½ cup sliced green onions
10 slices bacon, crisp-cooked and crumbled
  2 tablespoons chopped fresh basil leaves (optional)

1. Preheat oven to 400°F. On large baking sheet, arrange potatoes and bake 35 minutes or until tender. Let stand until cool enough to handle.

2. Cut each potato in half, then cut thin slice from bottom of each potato half. With small melon baller or spoon, scoop pulp from potatoes leaving ¼-inch shell. Place pulp in medium bowl; set shells aside.

3. Lightly mash pulp. Stir in remaining ingredients. Spoon or pipe potato filling into potato shells.

4. Arrange filled shells on baking sheet and broil 3 minutes or until golden and heated through. *Makes 30 bites*

Prep Time: 10 minutes
Cook Time: 40 minutes

Roasted Red Potato Bites

Quirky Bites

Porky Pinwheels

1 sheet frozen puff pastry, thawed
1 egg white, beaten
8 slices bacon, crisp-cooked and finely chopped
2 tablespoons packed brown sugar
¼ teaspoon ground red pepper

1. Place pastry onto piece of parchment paper. Brush surface with egg white.

2. Combine bacon, brown sugar and ground red pepper in small bowl. Sprinkle evenly over top; press lightly to adhere. Roll pastry jelly-roll style from long end. Wrap in parchment paper. Refrigerate 30 minutes.

3. Preheat oven to 400°F. Line baking sheet with parchment paper. Slice pastry into ½-inch-thick slices. Place 1 inch apart on prepared baking sheet.

4. Bake 10 minutes or until light golden brown. Remove to wire racks; cool completely.

Makes 24 pinwheels

Green Eggs

½ cup chopped green bell pepper
⅓ cup chopped parsley
3 tablespoons dill pickle relish
2 egg whites
1 teaspoon dried basil
1 teaspoon dried oregano
½ teaspoon salt
½ teaspoon black pepper
1 pound ground turkey
¼ cup uncooked oats
1 tablespoon olive oil
Hot Tomato Dipping Sauce (recipe follows)

1. Place bell pepper, parsley, relish, egg whites, basil, oregano, salt and black pepper in food processor or blender. Pulse until bell pepper is finely minced. Add turkey and oats; pulse 2 or 3 times or until just mixed. Chill mixture 15 minutes.

2. Preheat oven to 325°F. Shape mixture by tablespoonfuls into egg-shaped meatballs. Heat olive oil in nonstick skillet over medium heat. Brown meatballs on all sides. Place on nonstick baking sheet. Bake 10 to 15 minutes or until cooked through. Serve warm with dipping sauce.

Makes 16 meatballs

Hot Tomato Dipping Sauce

½ cup chopped tomato
½ cup vegetable broth or water
2 tablespoons tomato paste
1 teaspoon Italian seasoning
Hot pepper sauce (optional)

Combine tomato, broth, tomato paste and seasoning in small saucepan. Cook over low heat until just simmering. Season with hot pepper sauce, if desired. Serve with meatballs.

Green Eggs

Heavenly Ham Roll-Ups

1 package (9 ounces) OSCAR MAYER® Shaved Smoked Ham
5 tablespoons PHILADELPHIA® Light Cream Cheese Spread
15 asparagus spears (about 1 pound), trimmed

Preheat oven to 350°F. Flatten ham slices; pat dry. Stack ham in piles of 2 slices each; spread each stack with 1 teaspoon of the cream cheese spread.

Place 1 asparagus spear on one of the long sides of each ham stack; roll up. Place in 13×9-inch baking dish.

Bake 15 to 20 minutes or until heated through.   *Makes 15 servings, 1 roll-up each*

Prep Time: 15 minutes
Bake Time: 20 minutes

Parmesan-Pepper Crisps

2 cups (4 ounces) loosely packed coarsely grated Parmesan cheese
2 teaspoons black pepper

1. Preheat oven to 400°F. Line wire racks with paper towels.

2. Place heaping teaspoonfuls cheese 2 inches apart on ungreased nonstick baking sheet. Flatten cheese mounds slightly with back of spoon. Sprinkle each mound with pinch of pepper.

3. Bake 15 to 20 minutes or until crisps are very lightly browned. (Watch closely—crisps burn easily.) Cool 2 minutes on baking sheet. Carefully remove with spatula to prepared racks. Store in airtight container in refrigerator up to 3 days.   *Makes about 26 crisps*

Heavenly Ham Roll-Ups

Great Zukes Pizza Bites

    1 medium zucchini
    3 tablespoons pizza sauce
    2 tablespoons tomato paste
    1/4 teaspoon dried oregano
    3/4 cup (3 ounces) shredded mozzarella cheese
    1/4 cup shredded Parmesan cheese
    8 slices pitted black olives
    8 slices pepperoni

1. Preheat broiler; set rack 4 inches from heat.

2. Trim off and discard ends of zucchini. Cut zucchini into 16 (1/4-inch-thick) diagonal slices. Place on nonstick baking sheet.

3. Combine pizza sauce, tomato paste and oregano in small bowl; mix well. Spread scant teaspoon sauce over each zucchini slice. Combine cheeses in small bowl. Top each zucchini slice with 1 tablespoon cheese mixture, pressing down into sauce. Place 1 olive slice on each of 8 pizza bites. Place 1 folded pepperoni slice on each remaining pizza bite.

4. Broil 3 minutes or until cheese is melted. Serve immediately.   *Makes 8 servings*

Great Zukes Pizza Bites

Crispy Bacon Sticks

½ cup (1½ ounces) grated Wisconsin Parmesan cheese, divided
5 slices bacon, halved lengthwise
10 breadsticks

Microwave Directions

Spread ¼ cup cheese on plate. Press one side of bacon into cheese; wrap diagonally around breadstick with cheese-coated side toward stick. Place on paper plate or microwave-safe baking sheet lined with paper towels. Repeat with remaining bacon halves, cheese and breadsticks. Microwave on HIGH 4 to 6 minutes or until bacon is cooked, checking for doneness after 4 minutes. Roll again in remaining ¼ cup Parmesan cheese. Serve warm.

Makes 10 sticks

Favorite recipe from Wisconsin Milk Marketing Board

Tip Prepare these ahead of time and store in the refrigerator up to 4 hours. Microwave just before serving.

Crispy Bacon Sticks

California Ham Rolls

2 cups water

½ teaspoon salt, divided

1 cup short grain brown rice

2 tablespoons Asian rice vinegar* or cider vinegar

1 tablespoon sugar

4 (8×7-inch) sheets nori (sushi wrappers)*

8 thin strips ham (about 4 ounces)

¼ cup reduced-sodium soy sauce

1 tablespoon mirin (sweet rice wine)*

1 tablespoon minced chives

*These ingredients can be found in the Asian section of most supermarkets and in Asian specialty markets.

1. Bring water and ¼ teaspoon salt to a boil in medium saucepan over high heat. Stir in rice. Cover; reduce heat to low. Simmer 40 to 45 minutes or until water is absorbed and rice is tender but chewy. Spoon rice into large shallow bowl.

2. Combine vinegar, sugar and remaining ¼ teaspoon salt in small bowl. Microwave on HIGH 30 seconds. Stir to dissolve sugar. Pour over rice; mix well. Set aside to cool.

3. Place 1 sheet nori on work surface. Loosely spread about ½ cup rice over nori, leaving ½-inch border. Place 2 strips ham along width of nori. Roll up tightly into an 8-inch tube. Gently press tube to redistribute rice, if necessary. Cut tube into 6 slices with sharp knife. Place cut-side up on serving plate. Repeat with remaining nori, rice and ham.

4. Combine soy sauce and mirin in small bowl. Sprinkle with chives. Serve with ham rolls.

Makes 24 appetizers

California Ham Rolls

Summer Salad Lettuce Wraps

¼ cup extra-virgin olive oil
Juice of 1 lime
1 tablespoon red wine vinegar
1 cup grape tomatoes, halved
1 cup fresh corn
½ cup diced fresh mozzarella cheese
¼ cup diced red onion
¼ chopped fresh basil
Salt and black pepper
6 crunchy lettuce leaves

1. Whisk olive oil, lime juice and vinegar in large bowl.

2. Add tomatoes, corn, cheese, onion and basil; toss to coat. Season to taste with salt and pepper.

3. To serve, scoop ¼ cup salad mixture into each lettuce leaf; fold to eat.

Makes 3 servings

Summer Salad Lettuce Wrap

Bell Pepper Wedges with Herbed Goat Cheese

2 small red bell peppers
1 log (4 ounces) plain goat cheese, softened
⅓ cup whipped cream cheese
2 tablespoons minced fresh chives
1 teaspoon minced fresh dill
 Fresh dill sprigs (optional)

1. Cut off top quarter of bell peppers; remove core and seeds. Cut each pepper into 6 wedges. Remove ribs, if necessary.

2. Combine goat cheese, cream cheese, chives and minced dill in small bowl until well blended. Pipe or spread 1 tablespoon goat cheese mixture onto each pepper wedge. Garnish with dill sprigs, if desired.

Makes 6 servings

Tip Serve any remaining Herbed Goat Cheese with crackers or cucumber slices.

Bell Pepper Wedges with Herbed Goat Cheese

Guacamole Cones

6 (6-inch) flour tortillas
1 tablespoon vegetable oil
1 teaspoon chili powder
2 ripe avocados
1½ tablespoons fresh lime juice
1 tablespoon finely chopped green onion
¼ teaspoon salt
¼ teaspoon black pepper
    Dash hot pepper sauce (optional)
2 to 3 plum tomatoes, chopped

1. Preheat oven to 350°F. Line baking sheet with parchment paper.

2. Cut tortillas in half. Roll each tortilla half into cone shape; secure with toothpick. Brush outside of each cone with oil; sprinkle lightly with chili powder. Place on prepared baking sheet.

3. Bake 9 minutes or until cones are lightly browned. Turn cones upside down; bake about 5 minutes or until golden brown on all sides. Cool cones 1 minute; remove toothpicks and cool completely.

4. Cut avocados in half; remove and discard pits. Scoop avocado pulp from skins and place in medium bowl; mash with fork. Stir in lime juice, green onion, salt, pepper and hot pepper sauce, if desired, until blended.

5. Fill bottom of each tortilla cone with about 1 tablespoon chopped tomato; top with small scoop of guacamole and additional chopped tomatoes. Serve immediately.

Makes 12 cones

Guacamole Cones

Bavarian Pretzel Sandwiches

4 frozen soft pretzels, thawed or Soft Pretzels (page 18)
1 tablespoon German mustard
2 teaspoons mayonnaise
8 slices Black Forest ham
4 slices Gouda cheese
1 tablespoon water
  Coarse pretzel salt or kosher salt

1. Preheat oven to 350°F. Line baking sheet with parchment paper.

2. Carefully slice each pretzel in half crosswise using serrated knife. Combine mustard and mayonnaise in small bowl. Spread mustard mixture onto bottom halves of pretzels. Top with 2 slices ham, 1 slice cheese and top halves of pretzels.

3. Place sandwiches on prepared baking sheet. Brush tops of sandwiches with water; sprinkle with salt. Bake 8 minutes or until cheese is melted.

Makes 4 sandwiches

Bavarian Pretzel Sandwich

Hot and Spicy Hummus Dip

  1 container (8 ounces) prepared hummus
½ cup mayonnaise
  2 to 3 tablespoons chipotle salsa*
  1 tablespoon minced green onion
   Pita chips and/or vegetables

Chipotle salsa is a canned mixture of finely chopped chipotle peppers in adobo sauce. Look for it in the Latin foods section of the supermarket.

1. Combine hummus, mayonnaise, salsa and green onion in medium bowl. Refrigerate until ready to serve.

2. Serve with pita chips.

Makes about 6 servings

Prep Time: 5 minutes

Tip Use this spicy dip to liven up sandwiches or wraps.

Hot and Spicy Hummus Dip

Bite-You-Back Roasted Edamame

2 teaspoons vegetable oil
2 teaspoons honey
¼ teaspoon wasabi powder*
1 package (10 ounces) shelled edamame, thawed if frozen
Kosher salt

This ingredient can be found in the Asian section of most supermarkets and in Asian specialty markets.

1. Preheat oven to 375°F.

2. Combine oil, honey and wasabi powder in large bowl; mix well. Add edamame; toss to coat. Spread on baking sheet in single layer.

3. Bake 12 to 15 minutes or until golden brown, stirring once. Immediately remove from baking sheet to large bowl; sprinkle generously with salt. Cool completely before serving. Store in airtight container.

Makes 4 to 6 servings

Bite-You-Back Roasted Edamame

Spicy Polenta Cheese Bites

  3 cups water
  1 cup corn grits or cornmeal
½ teaspoon salt
¼ teaspoon chili powder
  1 tablespoon butter
¼ cup minced onion or shallot
  1 tablespoon minced jalapeño pepper*
½ cup (2 ounces) shredded sharp Cheddar cheese or fontina cheese

Jalapeño peppers can sting and irritate the skin, so wear rubber gloves when handling peppers and do not touch your eyes.

1. Grease 8-inch square baking pan. Bring water to a boil in large nonstick saucepan over high heat. Slowly add grits, stirring constantly. Reduce heat to low; cook and stir until grits are tender and water is absorbed. Stir in salt and chili powder.

2. Melt butter in small saucepan over medium-high heat. Add onion and jalapeño; cook and stir 3 to 5 minutes or until tender. Stir into grits; mix well. Spread in prepared pan. Let stand 1 hour or until cool and firm.

3. Preheat broiler. Cut polenta into 16 squares. Arrange squares on nonstick baking sheet; sprinkle with cheese. Broil 4 inches from heat 5 minutes or until cheese is melted and slightly browned. Remove immediately. Cut squares in half. Serve warm or at room temperature. (Polenta will firm as it cools.)

Makes 32 appetizers

Tip: For spicier flavor, add ⅛ to ¼ teaspoon red pepper flakes to the onion-jalapeño mixture.

Spicy Polenta Cheese Bites

Kiddie Creations

Snake Snacks

2 small ripe bananas
1 tablespoon fresh lemon juice
10 to 12 medium strawberries, hulled
2 small strawberries
1 slice kiwi (optional)

1. Cut bananas crosswise into ¼-inch slices. Place in medium bowl; toss gently with lemon juice to prevent bananas from turning brown.

2. Leave 2 medium strawberries whole; cut remaining medium strawberries crosswise into ¼-inch slices.

3. Place whole strawberries on serving plates for heads; alternate banana and strawberry slices behind heads to form snakes. Arrange small strawberries at end of snakes.

4. Cut 4 small pieces of banana for eyes; arrange on snake heads. Use toothpick to place kiwi seed in center of each eye, if desired.

Makes 2 servings

Tip: Try to choose strawberries that are about the same diameter as the banana so all the fruit slices that make up the snake will be close to the same width.

Chocolate Goldfish® Pretzel Clusters

1 package (12 ounces) semi-sweet chocolate pieces (about 2 cups)
2½ cups PEPPERIDGE FARM® Pretzel Goldfish® Crackers
1 container (4 ounces) multi-colored nonpareils

1. Line a baking sheet with waxed paper. Place the chocolate into a microwavable bowl. Microwave on HIGH for 1 minute. Stir. Microwave at 15 second intervals, stirring after each, until the chocolate is melted and smooth. Add the Goldfish® crackers and stir to coat.

2. Drop the chocolate mixture by tablespoonfuls onto the baking sheet. Sprinkle the clusters with the nonpareils.

3. Refrigerate for 30 minutes or until the clusters are firm. Store in the refrigerator.

Kitchen Tip: To wrap for gift-giving, arrange the clusters in small candy box lined with colored plastic wrap.   *Makes 1 pound*

Prep Time: 5 minutes
Cook Time: 1 minute
Chill Time: 30 minutes

Chocolate Goldfish® Pretzel Clusters

Friendly Face Pizzas

   3 whole wheat English muffins, split in half
   ¾ cup pasta sauce
   ¾ cup (3 ounces) shredded Italian cheese blend
    Assorted vegetables

1. Preheat oven to 400°F. Place English muffin halves on baking sheet.

2. Spread pasta sauce onto muffins. Sprinkle with cheese. Create silly faces on top of cheese with desired vegetables.

3. Bake 8 to 10 minutes or until cheese is melted. *Makes 6 servings*

Great Green Veggie Wedgies

   ½ cup whipped cream cheese
   2 (8- to 10-inch) spinach tortillas
   ¼ cup apricot or peach fruit spread
   ½ cup coarsely chopped fresh baby spinach
   ¼ cup grated carrot

1. Evenly spread cream cheese over one side of each tortilla.

2. Spread fruit spread over cream cheese on one tortilla. Sprinkle spinach and carrots over fruit spread.

3. Place the second tortilla, cheese side down, on top of the spinach and carrots. Lightly press tortillas together.

4. Cut the tortilla sandwich into 8 wedges. *Makes 2 servings*

Friendly Face Pizzas

Breakfast Mice

2 hard-cooked eggs, peeled and halved lengthwise
2 teaspoons mayonnaise
¼ teaspoon salt
2 radishes, thinly sliced and root ends reserved
8 raisins or currants
1 ounce Cheddar cheese, shredded or cubed
Spinach or lettuce leaves (optional)

1. Gently scoop egg yolks into small bowl. Mash yolks, mayonnaise and salt until smooth. Spoon yolk mixture back into egg halves. Place 2 halves, cut side down, on each serving plate.

2. Cut two tiny slits near the narrow end of each egg half; position 2 radish slices on each half for ears. Use the root end of each radish to form tails. Push raisins into each egg half to form eyes.

3. Place small pile of cheese in front of each mouse. Garnish with spinach.

Makes 2 servings

Breakfast Mice

Creepy Cobwebs

    4 to 5 cups vegetable oil, divided
    1 cup dry pancake mix
    ¾ cup plus 2 tablespoons milk
    1 egg, beaten
    ½ cup powdered sugar
    1 teaspoon ground cinnamon
    ½ teaspoon chili powder
    Dipping Sauce (recipe follows)

1. Pour 1 inch of oil into large deep skillet; heat to 350°F.

2. Combine pancake mix, milk, egg and 1 tablespoon oil in medium bowl. *Do not overmix.* Place 2 tablespoons batter into funnel or squeeze bottle; swirl into hot oil to form cobwebs. Cook until bubbles form. Gently turn using tongs and slotted spatula; cook 1 minute or until browned. Drain on paper towels.

3. Repeat with remaining batter. If necessary, add more oil to maintain 1-inch depth and heat oil to 350°F between batches.

4. Meanwhile, mix powdered sugar, cinnamon and chili powder in small bowl. Sprinkle over cobwebs. Serve cobwebs warm with Dipping Sauce. *Makes 10 to 12 servings*

Dipping Sauce

    1 cup maple syrup
    1 jalapeño pepper,* cored, seeded and minced

Jalapeño peppers can sting and irritate the skin, so wear rubber gloves when handling peppers and do not touch your eyes.

Combine syrup and jalapeño in small saucepan. Simmer 5 minutes or until syrup is heated through. Pour into heatproof bowl. *Makes 1 cup*

Creepy Cobwebs

Bird-wich

Mayonnaise or mustard
3 round slices deli meat
1 bottom half round sandwich bun
1 round sandwich bun, split
3 round slices cheese
2 leaves romaine lettuce
1 black olive
2 peas
Parsley sprigs (optional)

1. Layer mayonnaise and 2 slices deli meat on 1 bottom bun. Top with second bottom bun, mayonnaise, remaining slice deli meat and 1 slice cheese. Cut circle out of front end of top bun angling towards center of bun with round cutter. Spread mayonnaise on cut side of top bun and place on top of cheese.

2. For wings, insert 2 lettuce leaves between cheese and top bun on opposite sides of back of sandwich. For beak, cut 1 slice cheese in half. Loosely roll 1 half; roll other half slightly tighter and insert into looser half. Insert beak into hole in bun, cut sides in.

3. For eyes, cut olive in half crosswise. Attach to bun above beak with dabs of mayonnaise. Insert peas into holes in olives. For feet, cut 2 triangles out of remaining slice cheese. Cut 2 small V shapes out of short side of each triangle. Slide feet under sandwich, cut sides out.

4. Decorate sandwich with parsley sprigs for feathers. *Makes 1 sandwich*

Bird-wich

Bagel Dogs with Spicy Red Sauce

    1 cup ketchup
    1 medium onion, finely chopped
 ¼ cup packed brown sugar
    1 tablespoon cider vinegar
    2 teaspoons hot pepper sauce
    1 clove garlic, minced
    1 teaspoon Worcestershire sauce
    1 teaspoon liquid smoke (optional)
    4 bagel dogs

1. Combine all ingredients except bagel dogs in medium saucepan; bring to a boil over medium-high heat. Reduce heat; simmer 5 minutes, stirring occasionally.

2. Prepare bagel dogs according to package directions. Serve with sauce.

Makes 4 servings

Fried Pickle Spears

    3 tablespoons all-purpose flour
    1 teaspoon cornstarch
    3 eggs
    1 cup cornflake crumbs
 12 pickle spears, patted dry
 ½ cup vegetable oil

1. Line serving dish with paper towels; set aside. Combine flour and cornstarch in small bowl. Beat eggs in another small bowl. Place cornflake crumbs in third small bowl.

2. Coat pickle spears in flour mixture, shaking off excess. Dip pickle in eggs; roll in cornflake crumbs. Repeat with remaining pickles.

3. Heat oil in large nonstick skillet over medium heat. Cook four pickles at a time, 1 to 2 minutes per side or until golden brown. Remove to prepared serving dish. Repeat with remaining pickles.

Makes 4 servings

Bottom to top: Bagel Dogs with Spicy Red Sauce, Fried Pickle Spears

Indian Corn

¼ cup (½ stick) butter or margarine
1 package (10½ ounces) mini marshmallows
Yellow food coloring
8 cups peanut butter and chocolate puffed corn cereal
1 cup candy-coated chocolate pieces, divided
10 lollipop sticks*
Tan and green raffia*

Lollipop sticks and colored raffia are sold at craft and hobby stores.

1. Line large baking sheet with waxed paper; set aside.

2. Melt butter in large heavy saucepan over low heat. Add marshmallows; stir until melted and smooth. Tint with food coloring until desired shade is reached. Add cereal and ½ cup chocolate pieces; stir until evenly coated. Remove from heat.

3. With lightly greased hands, quickly divide mixture into 10 oblong pieces. Push lollipop stick halfway into each piece; shape like ear of corn. Place on prepared baking sheet. Press remaining ½ cup chocolate pieces into each ear. Let treats stand until set.

4. Tie or tape raffia to lollipop sticks to resemble corn husks.   *Makes 10 servings*

Indian Corn

Pig-wich

Mayonnaise or mustard
2 round slices deli meat
1½ round cheese slices, divided
1 leaf Boston lettuce
1 round sandwich bun, split
1 black olive
1 slice bologna
1 black bean

1. Layer mayonnaise, deli meat, 1 slice cheese and lettuce on bottom bun. Spread mayonnaise on cut side of top bun and place bun slightly off center on top of lettuce. For feet, slice olive in half lengthwise, then cut small V shape out of bottom of each half. Place olive halves on lettuce, cut side facing out.

2. For snout, cut circle from bologna with round cutter. Cut two small holes in circle just above center. Attach circle to top bun with dab of mayonnaise. For ears, cut two triangles out of bologna. Make two slits in top half of bun 1 inch apart and angling slightly towards sides of bun. Insert triangles into slits.

3. For eyes, cut out two small circles from remaining ½ slice cheese; attach to bun between ears and nose with dabs of mayonnaise. Cut black bean in half; attach cut sides to each cheese circle. For tail, cut long tapered slice of bologna. Attach tail to side of pig and curl.

Makes 1 sandwich

Pig-wich

Quicksand

¾ cup creamy peanut butter
5 ounces cream cheese, softened
1 cup pineapple preserves
⅓ cup milk
1 teaspoon Worcestershire sauce
Dash hot pepper sauce (optional)
1 can (7 ounces) refrigerated breadstick dough (6 breadsticks)
5 rich round crackers, crushed
Cut-up vegetables and fruit for dipping

1. Combine peanut butter and cream cheese in large bowl until well blended. Stir in preserves, milk, Worcestershire and hot pepper sauce, if desired. Transfer to serving bowl or spread in 8- or 9-inch glass pie plate. Cover with plastic wrap; refrigerate until ready to serve.

2. Preheat oven to 375°F. Cut each breadstick in half crosswise; place on ungreased baking sheet. Make 3 slits in one short end of each breadstick half to resemble fingers. Cut small piece of dough from other short end; press dough piece into hand to resemble thumb. Bake 8 to 10 minutes or until golden brown.

3. Just before serving, sprinkle dip with cracker crumbs; serve with breadstick hands, vegetables and fruit.

Makes 12 to 16 servings

Quicksand

Magic Rainbow Pops

1 envelope ($\frac{1}{4}$ ounce) unflavored gelatin
$\frac{1}{4}$ cup cold water
$\frac{1}{2}$ cup boiling water
1 carton (6 ounces) raspberry or strawberry yogurt
1 carton (6 ounces) lemon or orange yogurt
1 small can ($8\frac{1}{4}$ ounces) apricots or peaches with juice
Popsicle molds

1. Combine gelatin and cold water in 2-cup glass measuring cup. Let stand 5 minutes to soften. Add boiling water. Stir until gelatin is completely dissolved. Cool slightly.

2. For first layer, combine raspberry yogurt and $\frac{1}{4}$ cup gelatin mixture in small bowl; stir until completely blended. Fill each popsicle mold about one third full with raspberry mixture.* Freeze 30 to 60 minutes or until slightly frozen.

3. For second layer, combine lemon yogurt with $\frac{1}{4}$ cup gelatin mixture in small bowl; stir until completely blended. Pour lemon mixture over raspberry layer in each mold.* Freeze 30 to 60 minutes or until slightly frozen.

4. Place apricots with juice and remaining $\frac{1}{4}$ cup gelatin mixture in blender. Process 20 seconds or until smooth. Pour apricot mixture into each mold.* Cover each pop with mold top; freeze 2 to 5 hours or until pops are firm.

5. To remove pops from molds, place bottom of pop under warm running water for 2 to 3 minutes. Press firmly on bottom to release. (Do not twist or pull the popsicle stick.)

Makes about 6 pops

Pour any extra mixture into small paper cups. Freeze as directed in the tip.

Tip: Three-ounce paper cups can be used in place of the molds. Make the layers as directed or put a single flavor in each cup. Freeze cups about 1 hour, then insert wooden stick (which can be found at craft stores) into the center of each cup. Freeze completely. Peel cup off each pop to serve.

Magic Rainbow Pops

Candy Corn by the Slice

1 package (about 14 ounces) refrigerated pizza crust dough
½ cup (2 ounces) shredded mozzarella cheese
2 cups (8 ounces) shredded Cheddar cheese, divided
⅓ cup pizza sauce

1. Preheat oven to 400°F. Spray 13-inch round pizza pan with nonstick cooking spray. Press dough into pan.

2. Sprinkle mozzarella in 4-inch circle in center of pizza dough. Sprinkle 1 cup Cheddar cheese in 3-inch ring around center circle. Spoon pizza sauce over Cheddar cheese. Create 1½-inch border around edge of pizza with remaining 1 cup Cheddar cheese.

3. Bake 12 to 15 minutes or until edge is lightly browned and cheese is melted and bubbling. Cut into wedges.

Makes 8 slices

 **Tip** Keeping a couple packages of pizza crust dough on hand is a great way to make sure that a fun snack is only minutes away.

Candy Corn by the Slice

Sweet Surprises

Sweet Sushi

    1 package (10½ ounces) marshmallows
    3 tablespoons butter
    6 cups crisp rice cereal
       Green fruit roll-ups
       Candy fish
       Sliced strawberries, peaches and kiwi

1. Spray 13×9-inch baking pan and spatula with nonstick cooking spray.

2. Place marshmallows and butter in large microwavable bowl; microwave on HIGH 1 to 2 minutes or until melted and smooth, stirring once. Immediately stir in cereal until coated. Press mixture into prepared pan using waxed paper to press into even layer. Let stand 10 minutes.

3. Cut half of cereal bars into 2×1-inch rectangles; round edges of rectangles slightly with hands to form ovals. Cut remaining half of bars into 1½- to 2-inch circles using greased cookie or biscuit cutter.

4. Cut fruit roll-ups into ½-inch-wide and 1-inch-wide strips. Top ovals with candy or fruit; wrap with ½-inch fruit roll-up strips as shown in photo. Wrap 1-inch strips around circles; top with fruit or candy.

Makes 3 to 4 dozen pieces

Banana Split Cups

1 package (18 ounces) refrigerated chocolate chip cookie dough
2/3 cup "M&M's"® Chocolate Mini Baking Bits, divided
1 ripe medium banana, cut into 18 slices and halved
3/4 cup chocolate syrup, divided
2 1/4 cups any flavor ice cream, softened
Aerosol whipped topping
1/4 cup chopped maraschino cherries

Lightly grease 36 (1¾-inch) mini muffin cups. Cut dough into 36 equal pieces; roll into balls. Place 1 ball in bottom of each muffin cup. Press dough onto bottoms and up sides of muffin cups; chill 15 minutes. Press ⅓ cup "M&M's"® Chocolate Mini Baking Bits into bottoms and sides of dough cups. Preheat oven to 350°F. Bake cookies 8 to 9 minutes. Cookies will be puffy. Remove from oven; gently press down center of each cookie. Return to oven 1 minute. Cool cookies in muffin cups 5 minutes. Remove to wire racks; cool completely. Place 1 banana half slice in each cookie cup; top with ½ teaspoon chocolate syrup. Place about ½ teaspoon "M&M's"® Chocolate Mini Baking Bits in each cookie cup; top with 1 tablespoon ice cream. Top each cookie cup with ½ teaspoon chocolate syrup, whipped topping, remaining "M&M's"® Chocolate Mini Baking Bits and 1 maraschino cherry piece. Store covered in freezer.

Makes 3 dozen cookies

Banana Split Cups

Pretzel Fried Eggs

24 (1-inch) pretzel rings
1 cup white chocolate chips
24 yellow candy-coated chocolate pieces

1. Line baking sheet with waxed paper. Place pretzel rings about 2 inches apart on prepared baking sheet.

2. Place white chocolate chips in medium resealable food storage bag; seal bag. Microwave on HIGH 30 seconds. Knead bag gently and microwave 30 seconds more. Repeat until chips are melted. Cut ¼-inch corner from bag.

3. Squeeze chocolate from bag into center of each pretzel ring in circular motion. Finish with ring of chocolate around edge of pretzel. Use tip of small knife to smooth chocolate, if necessary. Place candy piece in center of each pretzel. Allow to harden at room temperature or refrigerate until set. Store in single layer in airtight container up to 1 week.

Makes 2 dozen eggs

Variation: To make "green eggs and ham," use green candy-coated chocolate pieces for yolks. Cut small pieces of pink fruit leather for ham. Serve 2 Pretzel Fried Eggs with small strips of fruit leather ham and square cinnamon cereal for toast.

Pretzel Fried Eggs

Marty the "Mousse"

WHAT YOU NEED

2 packages (8 squares each) BAKER'S® Semi-Sweet Chocolate, divided
1 package (8 ounces) PHILADELPHIA® Cream Cheese, softened
½ cup PLANTERS® Walnut Halves
Decorations: red candy-coated chocolate pieces and small candies

MAKE IT

MELT 8 chocolate squares. Beat cream cheese with mixer until creamy. Blend in melted chocolate. Refrigerate 1 hour or until firm.

SHAPE into 18 balls, using 4 teaspoons chocolate mixture for each; place in single layer on waxed paper-covered baking sheet.

MELT remaining chocolate squares. Dip balls in chocolate, 1 at a time, turning to evenly coat each ball. Return to baking sheet.

PRESS 2 nuts into top of each ball for the moose's antlers. Add decorations for the nose and eyes. Refrigerate until chocolate is firm. *Makes 18 servings*

Special Extra: Add 1 to 2 teaspoons of your favorite extract, such as peppermint, rum or almond, to chocolate mixture before shaping into balls.

Prep Time: 20 minutes (plus refrigerating)

Marty the "Mousse"

Chocolate Panini Bites

¼ cup chocolate hazelnut spread
4 slices hearty sandwich bread or Italian bread
Nonstick cooking spray

1. Preheat indoor grill.* Spread chocolate hazelnut spread evenly over two slices bread; top with remaining slices.

2. Spray sandwiches lightly with nonstick cooking spray. Grill 2 to 3 minutes or until bread is golden brown. Cut sandwiches into triangles.   *Makes 4 servings*

Panini can also be made on the stove in a ridged grill pan or in a nonstick skillet. Cook sandwiches over medium heat about 2 minutes per side.

Chocolate Raspberry Panini Bites: Spread 2 slices bread with raspberry jam or preserves. Spread remaining slices with chocolate hazelnut spread. Cook sandwiches as directed above. *Watch closely because jam burns easily.*

Mini S'mores Pies

6 mini graham cracker pie crusts
½ cup semisweet chocolate chips, divided
¾ cup mini marshmallows

1. Preheat oven to 325°F. Place pie crusts on baking sheet.

2. Divide ¼ cup chocolate chips between pie crusts. Sprinkle marshmallows over chocolate chips. Top with remaining ¼ cup chocolate chips.

3. Bake 3 to 5 minutes or until marshmallows are light golden brown.   *Makes 6 servings*

Chocolate Panini Bites

Chocolate-Covered Banana Pops

3 ripe large bananas

9 wooden popsicle sticks

2 cups (12-ounce package) HERSHEY'S SPECIAL DARK® Chocolate Chips or
    HERSHEY'S Semi-Sweet Chocolate Chips

2 tablespoons shortening (do not use butter, margarine, spread or oil)

1½ cups coarsely chopped unsalted, roasted peanuts

1. Peel bananas; cut each into thirds. Insert a wooden stick into each banana piece; place on wax paper-covered tray. Cover; freeze until firm.

2. Place chocolate chips and shortening in medium microwave-safe bowl. Microwave at MEDIUM (50%) 1½ to 2 minutes or until chocolate is melted and mixture is smooth when stirred.

3. Remove bananas from freezer just before dipping. Dip each piece into warm chocolate, covering completely; allow excess to drip off. Immediately roll in peanuts. Cover; return to freezer. Serve frozen.

Makes 9 pops

Variation: HERSHEY'S Milk Chocolate Chips or HERSHEY'S Mini Chips Semi-Sweet Chocolate may be substituted for HERSHEY'S SPECIAL DARK Chocolate Chips or HERSHEY'S Semi-Sweet Chocolate Chips.

Chocolate-Covered Banana Pops

Pound Cake Dip Sticks

½ cup raspberry jam, divided
1 package (10¾ ounces) frozen pound cake
1½ cups cold whipping cream

1. Preheat oven to 400°F. Spray baking sheet with nonstick cooking spray. Microwave ¼ cup jam on HIGH 30 seconds or until smooth.

2. Cut pound cake into 10 (½-inch) slices. Brush one side of slices lightly with warm jam. Cut each slice lengthwise into 3 sticks. Place sticks, jam side up, on prepared baking sheet. Bake 10 minutes or until cake sticks are crisp and light golden brown. Remove to wire rack.

3. Meanwhile, beat whipping cream in large bowl with electric mixer until soft peaks form. Add remaining ¼ cup raspberry jam; beat until combined. Serve pound cake dip sticks with raspberry whipped cream.

Makes 8 to 10 servings

Chocolate Spiders

1 package (12 ounces) semisweet chocolate chips
1 cup butterscotch chips
¼ cup (½ stick) butter
¼ cup creamy peanut butter
4 cups crisp rice cereal
Chow mein noodles and assorted candies

1. Line baking sheet with waxed paper.

2. Combine chocolate chips, butterscotch chips and butter in large saucepan; stir over medium heat until chips are melted and mixture is well blended. Remove from heat. Add peanut butter; mix well. Add cereal; stir to evenly coat.

3. Drop mixture by tablespoonfuls onto prepared baking sheet; insert chow mein noodles for legs and add candies for eyes.

Makes about 3 dozen

Doughnut Hole Spiders: Substitute chocolate-covered doughnut holes for shaped cereal mixture. Insert black string licorice, cut into 1½-inch lengths, into doughnut holes for legs. Use desired color decorating icing for eyes.

Pound Cake Dip Sticks

Cinnamon-Spice Dip

WHAT YOU NEED

$\frac{1}{4}$ cup packed brown sugar

$\frac{1}{8}$ teaspoon ground cinnamon

$\frac{1}{8}$ teaspoon ground nutmeg

2 cups thawed COOL WHIP® Whipped Topping

MAKE IT

STIR sugar and spices into COOL WHIP® until well blended.

REFRIGERATE 1 hour.

SERVE with strawberries, apple slices, assorted NABISCO® Cookies and HONEY MAID® Grahams Sticks. *Makes 13 servings, about 2 tablespoons each*

Special Extra: Garnish dip with a light sprinkling of additional cinnamon just before serving.

Prep Time: 10 minutes (plus refrigerating)

Cinnamon-Spice Dip

Mini Dessert Burgers

  1 box (12 ounces) vanilla wafer cookies,* divided
½ cup powdered sugar
¼ teaspoon salt
¾ cup NESTLÉ® TOLL HOUSE® Semi-Sweet Chocolate Morsels
⅓ cup milk
½ cup sweetened flaked coconut
½ teaspoon water
  3 drops green food coloring
    Red and yellow decorating gels (for ketchup and mustard)
  1 teaspoon melted butter (optional)
  1 tablespoon sesame seeds (optional)

*A 12-ounce box of vanilla wafers contains about 88 wafers.

RESERVE 48 wafers for bun tops and bottoms.

PLACE remaining wafers in large resealable bag. Crush into small pieces using a rolling pin. Combine wafer crumbs (about 1½ cups) with powdered sugar and salt in medium bowl.

MICROWAVE morsels and milk in medium, uncovered, microwave-safe bowl on HIGH (100%) power for 45 seconds; stir. If necessary, microwave at additional 10- to 15-second intervals, stirring just until smooth.

POUR chocolate mixture into wafer mixture; stir until combined. Cool for 10 minutes. Line baking sheet with wax paper. Roll mixture into 24 (1-inch) balls, about 1 tablespoon each. Place each ball on prepared sheet; flatten slightly to form burger patties.

COMBINE coconut, water and green food coloring in small, resealable plastic bag. Seal bag and shake to coat evenly with color.

PLACE 24 wafers, rounded side down, on prepared baking sheet. Top each wafer with 1 burger patty. Top each burger patty with 1 teaspoon colored coconut. Squeeze decorating gels on top of coconut. Top with remaining wafers. Brush tops of wafers with melted butter and sprinkle with sesame seeds, if desired.   *Makes 24 servings*

Mini Dessert Burgers

S'more Snack Cake

1 package (about 18 ounces) yellow cake mix, plus ingredients to prepare mix
1 cup chocolate chunks, divided
2½ cups bear-shaped graham crackers, divided
1½ cups mini marshmallows

1. Preheat oven to 350°F. Grease 13×9-inch baking pan.

2. Prepare cake mix according to package directions, adding ½ cup chocolate chunks and 1 cup graham crackers. Spread batter in prepared pan.

3. Bake 30 minutes. Remove cake from oven; sprinkle with remaining ½ cup chocolate chunks and marshmallows. Arrange remaining 1½ cups graham crackers evenly over top.

4. Return cake to oven; bake 8 minutes or until marshmallows are golden brown. Cool completely before cutting.

Makes 24 servings

 *Tip* This cake is best served the day it is made. Keep leftovers in an airtight container.

S'more Snack Cake

Drizzled Party Popcorn

  8 cups popped popcorn
  ½ cup HERSHEY'S Milk Chocolate Chips
  ½ cup REESE'S® Peanut Butter Chips
  2 teaspoons shortening (do not use butter, margarine, spread or oil)

1. Line cookie sheet or jelly-roll pan with waxed paper. Spread popcorn in thin layer on prepared pan.

2. Place milk chocolate chips and 1 teaspoon shortening in microwave-safe bowl. Microwave at MEDIUM (50%) 1 minute; stir. If necessary, microwave at MEDIUM an additional 15 seconds at a time, stirring after each heating, until chips are melted and smooth when stirred. Drizzle over popcorn.

3. Place peanut butter chips and remaining 1 teaspoon shortening in separate microwave-safe bowl. Microwave at MEDIUM 1 minute; stir. If necessary, microwave at MEDIUM an additional 15 seconds at a time, stirring after each heating, until chips are melted and smooth when stirred. Drizzle over popcorn.

4. Allow drizzle to set up at room temperature or refrigerate about 10 minutes or until firm. Break popcorn into pieces.   *Makes about 8 cups popcorn*

Notes: Popcorn is best eaten the same day it is prepared, but it can be stored in an airtight container. Recipe amounts can be changed to match your personal preferences.

Drizzled Party Popcorn

Acknowledgments

The publisher would like to thank the companies listed below for the use of their recipes and photographs in this publication.

Campbell Soup Company

Dole Food Company, Inc.

Heinz North America

The Hershey Company

JOLLY TIME® Pop Corn

© 2010 Kraft Foods, KRAFT, KRAFT Hexagon Logo, PHILADELPHIA AND PHILADELPHIA Logo are registered trademarks of Kraft Foods Holdings, Inc. All rights reserved.

© Mars, Incorporated 2010

Nestlé USA

Ortega®, A Division of B&G Foods, Inc.

Recipes courtesy of the Reynolds Kitchens

Unilever

Wisconsin Milk Marketing Board

METRIC CONVERSION CHART

VOLUME MEASUREMENTS (dry)

1/8 teaspoon = 0.5 mL
1/4 teaspoon = 1 mL
1/2 teaspoon = 2 mL
3/4 teaspoon = 4 mL
1 teaspoon = 5 mL
1 tablespoon = 15 mL
2 tablespoons = 30 mL
1/4 cup = 60 mL
1/3 cup = 75 mL
1/2 cup = 125 mL
2/3 cup = 150 mL
3/4 cup = 175 mL
1 cup = 250 mL
2 cups = 1 pint = 500 mL
3 cups = 750 mL
4 cups = 1 quart = 1 L

VOLUME MEASUREMENTS (fluid)

1 fluid ounce (2 tablespoons) = 30 mL
4 fluid ounces (1/2 cup) = 125 mL
8 fluid ounces (1 cup) = 250 mL
12 fluid ounces (1 1/2 cups) = 375 mL
16 fluid ounces (2 cups) = 500 mL

WEIGHTS (mass)

1/2 ounce = 15 g
1 ounce = 30 g
3 ounces = 90 g
4 ounces = 120 g
8 ounces = 225 g
10 ounces = 285 g
12 ounces = 360 g
16 ounces = 1 pound = 450 g

DIMENSIONS

1/16 inch = 2 mm
1/8 inch = 3 mm
1/4 inch = 6 mm
1/2 inch = 1.5 cm
3/4 inch = 2 cm
1 inch = 2.5 cm

OVEN TEMPERATURES

250°F = 120°C
275°F = 140°C
300°F = 150°C
325°F = 160°C
350°F = 180°C
375°F = 190°C
400°F = 200°C
425°F = 220°C
450°F = 230°C

BAKING PAN SIZES

Utensil	Size in Inches/Quarts	Metric Volume	Size in Centimeters
Baking or	8 × 8 × 2	2 L	20 × 20 × 5
Cake Pan	9 × 9 × 2	2.5 L	23 × 23 × 5
(square or	12 × 8 × 2	3 L	30 × 20 × 5
rectangular)	13 × 9 × 2	3.5 L	33 × 23 × 5
Loaf Pan	8 × 4 × 3	1.5 L	20 × 10 × 7
	9 × 5 × 3	2 L	23 × 13 × 7
Round Layer	8 × 1½	1.2 L	20 × 4
Cake Pan	9 × 1½	1.5 L	23 × 4
Pie Plate	8 × 1¼	750 mL	20 × 3
	9 × 1¼	1 L	23 × 3
Baking Dish	1 quart	1 L	—
or Casserole	1½ quart	1.5 L	—
	2 quart	2 L	—